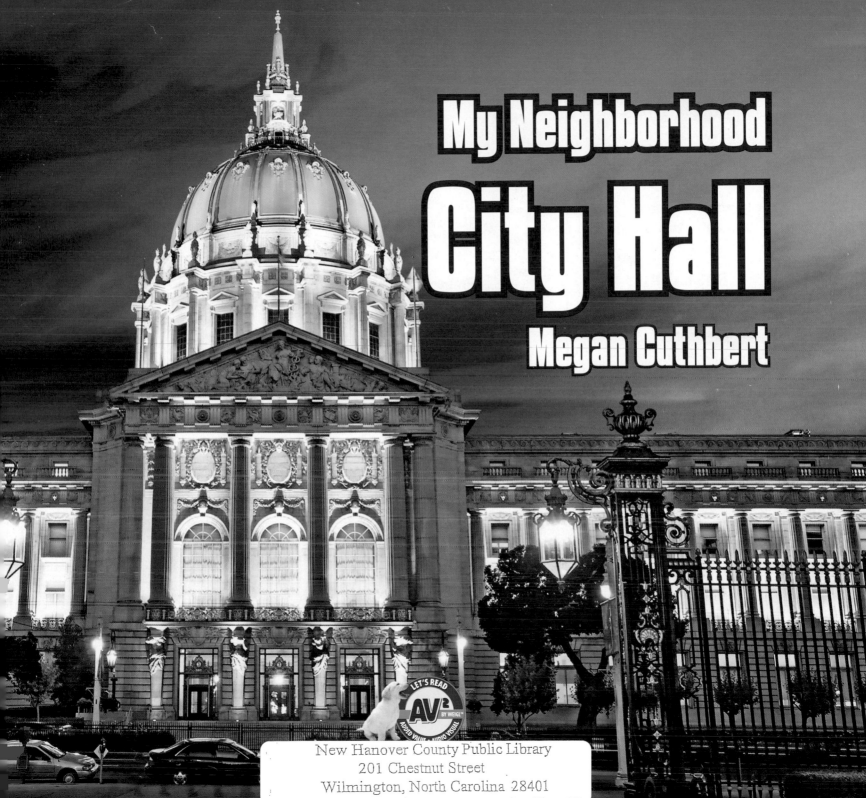

My Neighborhood
City Hall

Megan Cuthbert

Go to **www.av2books.com**, and enter this book's unique code.

BOOK CODE

Y108705

AV² by Weigl brings you media enhanced books that support active learning.

AV² provides enriched content that supplements and complements this book. Weigl's AV² books strive to create inspired learning and engage young minds in a total learning experience.

Your AV² Media Enhanced books come alive with...

Audio
Listen to sections of the book read aloud.

Video
Watch informative video clips.

Embedded Weblinks
Gain additional information for research.

Try This!
Complete activities and hands-on experiments.

Key Words
Study vocabulary, and complete a matching word activity.

Quizzes
Test your knowledge.

Slide Show
View images and captions, and prepare a presentation.

... and much, much more!

Published by AV² by Weigl
350 5th Avenue, 59th Floor New York, NY 10118
Websites: www.av2books.com   www.weigl.com

Library of Congress Control Number: 2014940882

ISBN 978-1-4896-1310-3 (hardcover)
ISBN 978-1-4896-1311-0 (softcover)
ISBN 978-1-4896-1312-7 (single user eBook)
ISBN 978-1-4896-1313-4 (multi-user eBook)

Printed in the United States of America in North Mankato, Minnesota
1 2 3 4 5 6 7 8 9 0 18 17 16 15 14

052014
WEP150314

Project Coordinators: Heather Kissock and Katherine Balcom
Design: Mandy Christiansen

Every reasonable effort has been made to trace ownership and to obtain permission to reprint copyright material. The publishers would be pleased to have any errors or omissions brought to their attention so that they may be corrected in subsequent printings.

Weigl acknowledges Getty Images as the primary image supplier for this title.

City Hall

CONTENTS

This is my neighborhood.

City hall is in my neighborhood.

City hall is a place where laws are made for my city.

Laws are made so we can live together as neighbors.

The mayor works in city hall and goes to special events in my neighborhood.

The mayor makes sure that the city is a nice place to live and to visit.

The mayor and the city council work together to help the city grow.

They decide where to put new schools and houses in the city.

The police, firefighters, and paramedics all work for the city.

They help keep my neighborhood safe.

City hall runs the buses and trains in the city.

City buses and trains help me get to the places that I want to go.

My family can go to city hall to get a new tag for my pet.

A tag helps people find my pet if it gets lost.

People in my neighborhood can go to city hall to talk about new ideas.

They meet with the mayor and the council.

Ron Moeser
Councillor Ward 44
Scarborough East

Mary Fragedakis
Councillor Ward 29
Toronto Danforth

Paula Fl...
Council...
Toronto-...

Vincent Crisanti
Councillor Ward 1
Etobicoke North

Frances Nunziata
Councillor Ward 11
York South-
Weston

Cesar Palacio
Councillor Ward 17
Davenport

Gloria Lindsay Luby
Councillor Ward 4
Etobicoke Centre

Giorgio Mamm...
Councillor Ward...
York West

My class visits city hall to meet the mayor.

We see the room where the city council works.

See what you have learned about city hall.

Which of these pictures does not show a city hall?

KEY WORDS

Research has shown that as much as 65 percent of all written material published in English is made up of 300 words. These 300 words cannot be taught using pictures or learned by sounding them out. They must be recognized by sight. This book contains 50 common sight words to help young readers improve their reading fluency and comprehension. This book also teaches young readers several important content words, such as proper nouns. These words are paired with pictures to aid in learning and improve understanding.

Page	Sight Words First Appearance
4	is, my, this
5	in
6	a, are, city, for, made, place, where
7	as, can, live, so, the, there, together, we
8	and, to, the, works
9	makes, that
10	grow, help
11	houses, new, put, schools, they
12	all
13	keep
14	runs
15	get, go, I, me, want
16	family
17	find, if, it, people
18	about, ideas, talk
19	with
21	see

Page	Content Words First Appearance
4	neighborhood
5	city hall
6	laws
7	neighbors
8	mayor, events
10	city council
12	firefighters, police, paramedics
14	buses, trains
16	pet, tag
19	council
20	class
21	lost

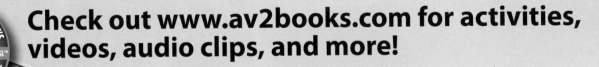

ML   7-15